To my little helpers, Jay and Ben.

Happy Christmas! Love Daddy

~ M M

LITTLE TIGER PRESS
1 The Coda Centre, 189 Munster Road, London SW6 6AW
www.littletiger.co.uk

First published in Great Britain 2015
This edition published 2015

Copyright © Little Tiger Press 2015
Text by Clement C. Moore
Illustrations copyright © Mark Marshall 2015
Mark Marshall has asserted his right to be identified as the illustrator of this work
under the Copyright, Designs and Patents Act, 1988

Printed in China • LTP/1400/1154/0615
2 4 6 8 10 9 7 5 3 1

This Little Tiger book
belongs to:

_____

_____

_____

The Night Before Christmas

Clement C. Moore

Mark Marshall

LITTLE TIGER PRESS
London

'Twas the night before Christmas,
when all through the house
Not a creature was stirring,
not even a mouse.

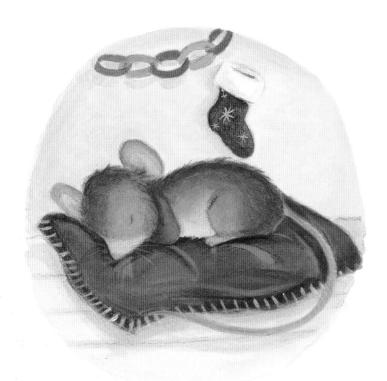

The stockings were hung
by the chimney with care,
In hopes that
St Nicholas
soon would be there.

Us children were nestled
all snug in our beds,
While visions of
s u g a r - p l u m s
danced in our heads.

And Mamma in her 'kerchief, and Dada in his cap,
Had just settled down for a long winter's nap.

When out on the lawn
there arose such a
c l a t t e r,
I sprang from the bed
to see what was the matter.

Away to the window
I flew like a flash,
Tore open the shutters
and threw up the sash.

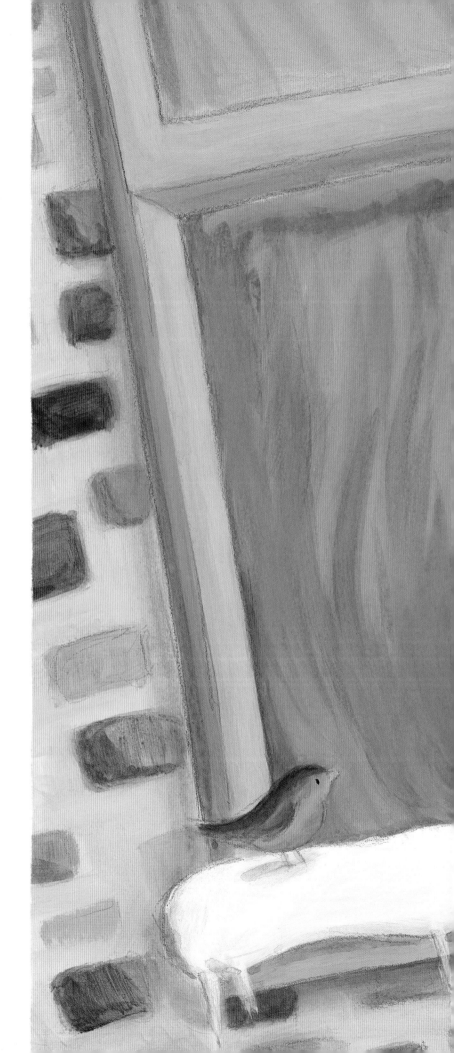

The moon on the breast of the new-fallen snow
Gave the lustre of mid-day to objects below.
When, what to my wondering eyes should appear,
But a miniature sleigh, and eight tiny reindeer.

With a little old driver, so lively and quick,
I knew in a moment it must be St Nick.
More rapid than eagles his coursers they came,
And he whistled, and shouted, and called them by name . . .

"Now Dasher, now Dancer, now Prancer, and Vixen! On Comet, on Cupid, on Donder and Blitzen!

To the top of the porch, to the top of the wall! Now dash away, dash away, dash away all!"

As dry leaves that before
the wild hurricane fly,
When they meet with an obstacle,
mount to the sky,

So up to the house top
the coursers they flew,
With the sleigh full of toys,
and St Nicholas too.

And then, in a twinkling, I heard on the roof
The **prancing** and **pawing** of each **little hoof**.

As I drew in my head, and was turning around,
Down the chimney St Nicholas came with a bound.

He was dressed all in fur, from his head to his foot,
And his clothes were all tarnished with ashes and soot.
A bundle of toys he had flung on his back,
And he looked like a peddler just opening his pack.

His eyes – how they **twinkled**! His dimples how **merry**!
His cheeks were like roses, his nose like a **cherry**!
His droll little mouth was drawn up like a bow,
And the beard of his chin was as
white as the snow.

The stump of a pipe he held tight in his teeth,
And the smoke it encircled his head like a wreath.
He had a broad face, and a little round belly,
That shook when he laughed like a bowlful of jelly.

He was chubby and plump,
a right jolly old elf,
And I laughed when I saw him,
in spite of myself.

A wink of his eye
and a twist of his head,
Soon gave me to know
I had nothing to dread.

He spoke not a word,
but went straight to his work,
And filled all the stockings,
then turned with a jerk.

And laying his finger
aside of his nose,
And giving a nod,
up the chimney
he rose.

He sprang to his sleigh, to his team gave a whistle,

And away they all flew like the down of a thistle.

But I heard him exclaim, 'ere he drove out of sight,

"Happy Christmas to all, and to all a good night!"

Books make the best stocking fillers!

When Granny SAVED Christmas

JULIA HUBERY   CAROLINE PEDLER

Is It Christmas Yet?

Jane Chapman

Silent Night

Juliet Groom
Tim Warnes

One Special Christmas

M Christina Butler   Tina Macnaughton

The Best Christmas Ever!

Marni McGee
Gavin Scott

Waiting for Santa

Steve Metzger   Alison Edgson

For information regarding any
of the above titles or for our catalogue,
please contact us:
Little Tiger Press, 1 The Coda Centre,
189 Munster Road, London SW6 6AW
Tel: 020 7385 6333
E-mail: contact@littletiger.co.uk
www.littletiger.co.uk